Living with Richard

Memories of a Marriage

By Marilynn Valentine Patrick

PublishAmerica
Baltimore

ISBN: 978-1-4489-7250-0
PUBLISHED BY PUBLISHAMERICA, LLLP
www.publishamerica.com
Baltimore

Printed in the United States of America

Dedication

FOR RICHARD

You were meant for me.

Special Thanks

To Jeff Wilson, who encouraged me to finish this manuscript and kindly read it a couple of times and offered suggestions. Jeff is a husband, father, doctor, pilot, and author. I am immensely humbled that he so willingly offered to mentor me.

To Marissa Patrick, my daughter-in-law and published poet, who assisted me in getting this book published.

To Krisanne Shields, for computer skills that allowed me to navigate the nether land of cyberspace and get the manuscript ready for publication on time.

To Marilyn Tirrell, a very special friend (but that is another story) who did an extraordinary job of editing the book for me.

To Thomas, Cindy, Megan, Ryan, Krisanne, Danny, Lynne, Matt, Zach, Christopher, Marissa, and Victoria who compose the current Patrick clan and all Patrick's yet to come and, of course, to Richard for putting up with me, lo, these many years. It's been a nasty job but someone had to do it.

AS LONG AS I LIVE

THE SUN THAT RISES,
THE MOON THAT SETS,
YESTERDAY'S SURPRISES
THAT LINGER YET.
ALL THAT THIS LIFE HAS TO GIVE,
THESE THINGS ARE MINE,
AS LONG AS I LIVE.

MARILYNN VALENTINE
1959

FOREWORD

From my earliest memory, I have always wanted to write a book. It was my desire that it would become a great American novel. I hate to tell you folks, it isn't. The only novel thing about this book is that our marriage has lasted so long.

All children should have the opportunity to know their grandparents. I never had the chance to know any of mine. For that very reason, I wanted to leave a part of Richard and me to the future Patrick generations. I wanted them to get to know us as real people; people who lived, loved, had the ups and downs that marriage brings, and who still managed to laugh along the way.

We have been blessed with four children and five grandchildren. The youngest grand is 12. All are old enough to remember us. When they grow old, it is my wish that they see us as people; not just grandma and grandpa.

Table of Contents

Living with Richard

Memories of a Marriage

A THING OF BEAUTY DOESN'T ALWAYS LAST FOREVER

I'm Marilynn and I'm old. I wasn't always old. The aging process amazes me! I'm positive that I was young when I went to bed last night. I'm just as certain that, as I slumbered, the Sandman got ticked off with someone and took it out on me. I fell into bed with a face that could launch a thousand ships and woke up with a face that couldn't dock a dinghy. Alright, so it wasn't that dramatic but it WAS bad.

I went to bed one night wanting to control my world and when I woke up, the only thing I desired to control was my bladder.

The aging process continues to amaze me.

For Example:
-   Halloween was an event that we donned costumes to attend. Now, I just go as a charpei.

-   People offer to pay you to keep your clothes on instead of begging you to take them off.
-   Your kids offer to send you on vacation. They even agree to let the grandchildren go with you.
-   You don't care how big your backside gets. Your neck is too stiff to check it out in a mirror.

The benefits go on and on. Unfortunately, my memory doesn't!

HERE COMES THE BRIDE

Richard and I were married in New Jersey on a dark and dismal day, July 12th, 1964.

Those who believe in superstition say that rain on your wedding day will bring good luck to the newlyweds until death do them part.

God, being all knowing, understood just how much luck we were going to need. He sent the bluebird of happiness to pay us a visit.

We didn't actually see the bird. We know he was there because he left us a sign. We found his purple blessing on the train of my wedding gown.

Several dry cleanings failed to remove the stain.

After a honeymoon trip to Niagara Falls, we lived in an apartment in Jersey City, NJ. I already mentioned that we needed more luck than most. After a very short time passed, we came to the realization that we should have rented an apartment with swinging doors. If I wasn't angry and leaving, he was.

Seventeen months later, we had our first child. Four and one half years later, we had four children; Thomas, Krisanne, Lynne, and Christopher. Life was good.

Richard worked the evening shift and a lot of overtime. I worked part time days. We didn't have an opportunity to spend a lot of time together; ergo, we didn't have much time to fuss and fight. Okay, we did, but we were both too tired to make it worthwhile.

The next twenty years passed as quickly as the flash of a firefly winking in the night.

After we hit fifty, we began to mellow. Our kids became adults and married and had kids of their own.

Richard joined a golf league and the pursuance of par. I've never understood why someone would want to be 'par' or 'below par.' Seems like an unnatural goal to me. I began hunting for treasures at antique stores and flea markets. We seldom saw one another until about 5:00 in the afternoon. We'd have dinner at a favorite restaurant and pick a movie we both wanted to see. That's how we would end our Saturdays.

We didn't recognize it at the time but, in retrospect, we enacted the courtship process all over again.

This time, when we fell in love, the love was for the new person we had helped each other to become. It was a love that allowed us to be the 'real' us and not what the other one thought we should be. I am not about to trick you into thinking that either of us were more lovable. Rather, we accepted each other, warts and all. No more, "You're not the boss of me" attitude that gets in the way in relationships.

As a result of our new found, mature love, I offer you an inside view of the Patrick evolution revolution.

THINGS THAT GO BUMP
IN THE NIGHT

Let's begin with the account of the one and only time Richard ever hit me. Don't be shocked. It happens in the best of marriages.

I was four months pregnant with our first child and he slugged me. Yep! I assure you this is the absolute truth. I wouldn't lie. What a monster! In the words of the late, great Paul Harvey, "Now, the rest of the story."

We only had one television. It was in the living room. Both of us had to rise early the next day to go to work. The TV set was turned off and while Richard went from room to room to turn out the lights and make certain the doors and windows were locked (did I mention we lived in New Jersey?), I headed to the bedroom.

A brilliant idea popped into my mind. I would hide behind a stand-alone cabinet in the kitchen and jump out and yell "Boo" when he walked by. Oh, boy, I was going to get him good!

The house was completely dark except for the street lights outside. When I heard his footsteps nearby, I jumped from my hiding place and screamed, "Boo!"

He must have thought I said, "Boom!" He hauled off and swung his fist at me. At the last second, something must have triggered in his brain. Before he sent me flying with a full fledged k.o., he recognized that it was me and managed to hold back enough so that he only grazed my chin.

He felt so badly. Only my pride was hurt but I've gotten a lot of mileage out of the story.

Every now and then, when I aggravate him, he will tell me to "Go hide."

WHAT'S IN A NAME?

We were thrilled when we learned that I was pregnant with our first child. Would it be a boy? Would it be a girl? Would it have brown eyes like Richard or green like mine? What would we name it?

What would we name it??

Richard is Polish. I'm a little bit of everything and, according to family lore, part Indian. Naming a child is a big deal. I mean, it sticks with the child for the rest of the child's life. We wanted to give our baby a name that suited him and one that would proudly reflect Richard's Polish heritage and my Indian blood.

It was as if we were both struck by a thunderbolt. We looked at each other and, at the exact same moment, the perfect name came to us...

"We'll call him Running Dummy!"

Get over it. It's just a joke. We named him Thomas Andrew after both of his Grandfathers.

BREAKFAST IS (ALWAYS) READY

I had always planned to breast feed my children. Breast feeding was not a common occurrence in the 1960's. If you nursed your baby it was considered a throw-back to the time when people could not afford bottles and formula. As ridiculous as this seems, it was a fact.

When the pediatrician I had chosen came to see me, the first words out of his mouth were, "Why are you nursing your baby?" Not, "Mrs. Patrick, you have a beautiful son;" no, "you have a healthy son;" not even a, "too bad he's bald." I explained my reasons. He left and I never saw him again. He did not have the courtesy to discharge Thomas. He never came back. My OB could discharge me, but the pediatrician had to discharge the baby.

A friend recommended a pediatrician who had recently begun his practice. Dr. Elkas was young and unmarried at the time but this was a good thing for me. He was aware that the medical community was beginning to extol the value of a mother's milk. He was wonderfully supportive.

When Thomas was about ten days old, my breasts became engorged and very sore. Where did I go for help? Young, unmarried Dr.Elkas. I reached his answering service (of course) and asked that they have him call me back.

A couple of hours later, the phone rang. I picked up and heard a man's voice and that's all I needed to hear. Assuming that it was Dr. Elkas returning my call, I didn't let him get "Mrs. Patrick?" uttered before I poured out all my aches, pains and frustration, asking him for advice and hoping for sympathy. A few minutes later, I had the good sense to shut up.

There were a few seconds of silence before the voice responded. "Mrs. Patrick, this is Mr. Leonard, your insurance man."

As you may have guessed, I did not die of embarrassment and successfully nursed all four of our children. Thanks, Dr. Elkas.

LABOR OF LOVE
OR LOVE OF LABOR?

Richard had never been around pregnant women and was woefully unprepared for the joys of pregnancy. Morning sickness was "all in the mind." HA! I proved him wrong time and time, and time and time, and time again. The one time I'm right and I couldn't enjoy the victory.

Other than the nausea and vomiting, the first three pregnancies were easy. The actual birth process was duck soup for me. Problems came from Richard's lack of labor education.

My water broke with Thomas. Phone cameras were a long way from reality in 1965. I would have loved to have had the capability to record him following me around with a mop and the dog following him and sniffing the floor. He was too busy worrying about a dirty floor to take me to the hospital.

He was at work when I went into labor with Krisanne and was difficult to track down.

Onset of labor with Lynne began at 1:30 in the morning and I could not wake him. The alarm shrilled at 5:30 a.m. and he responded accordingly.

Christopher is a whole 'nother story.

I was on the telephone with my friend, Linda, when my water broke. I explained to Linda what had happened and then called Richard at work. No answer. Tried several times with the same results. I called Linda back and asked her to please take me to his plant.

Picture this: A Ford station wagon with a woman driver, her four children, a very pregnant woman and her three children, and one angry cop.

In Endicott, Mercereau Street is a one-way street from 5:00-6:00 p.m. Don't ask me why; ask the angry cop. Linda is concentrating on her driving, I want to know "Where's Richard?" and the children are doing what seven children in a green Ford station wagon do. Use your visualization skills.

We hear the siren before we see the flash of the red lights. Uh-Oh. Cops are accustomed to danger, but this cop had no idea with what he was a-messin'. Linda provided her identification documents and tried her best to explain that she was enroute to the hospital with a woman about to give birth. Either he was deaf (maybe from the seven screaming kids) or thought he was

having a hallucination (maybe from the seven screaming kids) but he paid her no attention. Linda, a very patient woman, frustrated, interrupted his lecture and informed him, in no uncertain terms, "Officer, we have an emergency and this woman must get to the hospital."

He ended his verbal tirade to glance at me. The light bulb in his head must have switched on; unless he planned to deliver a baby, he should send us on our way.

We stopped by Richard's business and the entrance was locked. Richard was working overtime. No one responded to the bell or the banging on the door. I left a note on the windshield of the car that informed him to go straight to the hospital. I gave birth at 7:20 p.m. A tired man with a goofy smile on his face ambled into my room shortly after 8:00 p.m. It was my pragmatic husband who wanted to know, "Does this mean you don't need the car to go pick strawberries tomorrow?"

Linda, her husband Bill, our seven kids and I had planned to go pick strawberries the next day. Linda, who had allergies, would entertain the kids while Bill and I picked the berries.

The doctor nixed our plans.

I DIDN'T KNOW
THEY HAD MOVED 'EM

Our second child, Krisanne, was born in February, 1967. One of our favorite "embarrass your kids" stories is about her trip to the hospital for a tonsillectomy.

She and Thomas were scheduled to have their tonsils out on the same day. We left the two younger children with our friend, Linda Hart, and proceeded to the hospital.

Paper work was taken care of and pre-op shots given. THEN, the doctor decides to check their ears and throats. As fate would have it, Krisanne had an ear infection.

I took her back over to Linda's. As soon as we got in the door, she turned around, pulled down her panties, proudly displayed the needle mark on her bottom and said, "Mrs. Hart, look, I got my tonsils out."

SHE SAID...SHE SAID

Lynne Valentine arrived in September, 1968. She proved to be the easiest baby to care for thus far; at least for the first eighteen months. Thomas and Krisanne had both had colic and I used to walk the floor at midnight and cry with them.

It is impossible to pinpoint the exact day that Lynne decided it would be a challenge to lock horns with Mom two, three, or fifty times a day. For the next twenty years or so, if I said "black," she said "white." If I said "vanilla," she said "chocolate." If I said "yes, you will".........you get the picture.

One doesn't have to have a PhD. in psychology to know the eight words that were spoken and unspoken at least a dozen times a day. "I hope you have one just like you." Admit it. Be honest. Every parent in the world has thought, if not spoken, those eight words.

I'm here to admonish you to be careful what you ask

for. Lynne wasn't content to have one just like her. She had two. And then, she did the unthinkable. SHE MOVED BACK HOME!

Think before you speak, my friends.

Lynne and I are best friends today. Through all the craziness, we both always knew that we loved each other very much.

No matter what, Moms, hang in there. It's so sweet when your children not only love you, but finally grow to like you.

SAY WHAT?

One day, Thomas and Krisanne were watching 'Davy and Goliath', a children's program that was presented by the Lutheran church. The stories revolved around a boy and his dog and there was always a moral to the story.

During each of the programs there would be a 'Words from Unity' segment. A Bible scripture would appear on the TV screen. That particular Sunday, I Corinthians 13 was chosen. Krisanne, who was about six at the time began to read, "Love is kind, love is pa, pat, pati." As she was trying to sound out the word, seven year old Thomas, in an effort to display not only his superior word skills, but also his knowledge of God's word, piped up and said, "Love is patient, dummy."

Out of the mouth of babes..........

YOU CAN'T HAVE YOUR CAKE
AND JELLO TOO

Richard's mother and father were Polish. They had both been born in America but their parents were not. Richard's father was a little more worldly than his mother. She never traveled more than 200 miles from the place of her birth.

Richard had been reared in Garfield, New Jersey, which is pretty metropolitan. When we moved to New York and Richard began to hunt, like all mothers, she was very interested in his new hobby.

When they spoke during hunting season, she always wanted to know if he had shot any peasants or reindeer.

Ours kids thought Daddy was out there killing people and Santa's sled pullers.

Mom also was an avid reader, but not much of a TV fan.

She was a great cook and always made home made

chicken noodle soup (with home made noodles), stuffed chicken, kielbasa, pierogi and crischiki when we visited. Yum!

We usually made pigs of ourselves and didn't want dessert. Polish women are known for being food pushers. She insisted that we have cookies or cake. Richard told her, "No, Ma, I don't even have room for Jello."

She shot back with, "I don't have Jello, I have cookies or cake."

In case you are too young to remember, Bill Cosby did a Jello commercial and "No room for Jello" was the catch phrase.

She was a great mother-in-law. She taught me how to cook all of the above plus sauerkraut soup.

Recipe to follow.

BEWARE OF POLACKS
BEARING GIFTS

Richard, the children, and I would try to visit his parents in New Jersey every six weeks or two months. They did not like to travel.

One weekend, when we were visiting, Mom took Richard aside and gave him a twenty dollar bill and told him that she wanted him to buy Thomas a bike; and, oh, by the way, don't tell Pop she gave him the money.

Just before we left to head back to Endicott, Pop took Richard aside, gave him twenty dollars, and, oh, by the way, don't tell Mom.

Subterfuge is not generally a good thing.

Thomas got a new bike, and, within a week of getting this new bike, he got eight stitches in the chin and a broken jaw.

As far as I know, Mom never knew that Pop gave Richard money for the bike and Pop never knew that

Mom had given Richard any money for the bike. They both felt responsible for Thomas' injuries and were unable to tell each other why.

Oh what a tangled web we weave.

NOT ALL TURKEYS ARE BIRDS

Once we relocated from New Jersey to upstate New York, Richard became a hunter. He didn't succeed in his attempt to get a deer every year but that did not affect his resolve to try.

To fathom why anyone wants to go into the woods before sun-up, bundled in long johns, camouflage paint smeared over every exposed part of their body and sit on a three foot square tree stand ten feet above the ground, freezing, with no civilized bathroom in sight is beyond/below my level of intelligence. REAL hunters stay from dawn till sundown. If they are lucky (?) enough to get a deer, then they must drag it out of the woods. Men have been known to drag them miles.

Many of them go home to face wives and children who are less than thrilled to see Bambi dead.

Opening day of hunting season was the Monday before Thanksgiving and many guys took the day off

work. Friday after Thanksgiving was an even bigger day. Wives typically looked on Black Friday as a perfect day. Husbands loved their wives for not being on their backs about going and wives were glad that the husbands would still be out when they returned from shopping. We could bring in bags and bags of Christmas gifts and they would never see them until December 25th. Everybody's happy.

My friend, Paula Gardner, and I did our part to improve the economy. Pleased with our purchases, we went back to my house to relax. Busted! Richard and the two fellas he had hunted with were already home. Rats. No deer meant bad mood and bad mood meant shopping might be an issue.

Richard's friends will remain nameless. One was a cop and one was a preacher. None of them had bagged a deer but Richard had shot a wild turkey. A big, dirty, nasty, smelly turkey. The others guys decided leaving to be the better part of valor. The responsibility of cleaning the big, dirty, nasty, smelly turkey rested on Richard's shoulders. Meaning, my shoulders. He was a city boy and had never seen fowl dressed.

We had chickens when I was a kid so I knew you had to get the feathers off and the guts out.

My Mother would boil water and dip the bird in it. The hot bath water released the feathers. Our big, dirty, nasty, smelly turkey (future references to this creature will be b-d-n-s) didn't know we expected him to relinquish his plumes. I heated gallons of hot water, poured it into a new galvanized garbage can and repeated the cycle several time. Nightmare city. It took hours to rid that b-d-n-s bird of his epidermal growth. We won't talk about the pin feathers.

When we decided to eat the b-d-n-s turkey, we invited the preacher and his wife and the cop and his wife to dinner to share our trophy bird. The preacher's wife refused to come. Ahh! You are probably thinking that she is an animal lover or a tree hugger. I'm here to tell you she wasn't. In fact, she got a hunting license and shot her own deer. The fact of the matter is, she refused to eat it because it offended her conscience. The turkey had been shot out of season. He was illegal (to be more accurate, he was a dead turkey, not an ill eagle) so she would not share our bounty.

I asked Richard what possessed him to shoot something out of season. He shrugged his shoulders and replied, "The cop told me to shoot it and the preacher blessed it. Sounds like a righteous kill to me."

FOOTNOTE: If a loved one ever brings home a b-d-n-s turkey, SKIN IT!!!

JUST SAY "NO" TO DRUGS

Richard doesn't have a lot to say around people he doesn't know well. I'm the talker.

There was one day in particular that I wish he had chosen to keep that image intact. He had a tooth that was giving him trouble that he had to have extracted. We had a friend who was an oral surgeon who would put you to sleep for the procedure.

While the doctor is extracting the tooth, I get a call from the school. The nurse informed me that Christopher, who was in kindergarten at the time, had had an accident on the jungle gym in the playground and that he required stitches.

I go pick him up at school and take him back to the doctor's office. Oral surgeons can suture from the neck up. Christopher had managed to hit his chin on a bar on the jungle gym and put his teeth all the way through his bottom lip, requiring internal and external suturing.

Like most five year olds, he was hurt, he was scared, and he was crying. I kept trying to calm him down until we got back into the recovery area where they had Richard.

As soon as I walk in the room, Richard, in his semi-drugged state starts asking, "Hey, Marilynn, you want to get laid?" … Now, I'm trying to calm Christopher and I've got a loud, horny husband asking inappropriate questions in a doctor's office. I'm trying to shush Christopher and Richard.

When it became apparent that neither one was going to stop screaming, I began encouraging Christopher to scream as loud as he could to drown out his father's voice.

LEAVE THEM ALONE AND THEY'LL COME HOME, DRAGGIN' THEIR LAUNDRY BEHIND THEM

In the late 1970's and early '80's, a new mania struck middle class America. Camping. I won't even tell you how many of our friends bought pop-up campers or tents and took to the highways on week-ends and vacations.

To this day, at the advanced age of 68, I still am unable to figure out this phenomenon. Several thousand dollars for a camper, Coleman stoves, Coleman lanterns, mosquito nets, sleeping bags; money to fill the gas tank, bug spray and who knows what else. The open highways and the promise of bonfires, starry nights and spending time with others as nuts as you, call to you like Circe and her Sirens.

Answer me this. Why does any sane person waste a day packing a trailer, traveling who knows how far and for how long, set up tents or campers, go find firewood, start a fire and cook; walk as far as necessary to get water, wash dishes, or go to the bathroom (which you share with lots of people you don't know and definitely don't want the opportunity to know)? WHY go to all this trouble for a couple of days when it should be apparent that you will have to go home and unpack the camper, wash any linens used and pulling your dirty underwear behind you? It's also quite possible that you may have been eaten alive by black flies, or mosquitoes, suffering from sunburn or athletes' foot from the communal shower stalls.

Rational folks just don't do these things. Who, in their right mind, would opt to leave a perfectly lovely home with hot and cold running water, gas and electricity, heat or air conditioning and, best of all, a bathroom/shower that does not have to be shared with strangers who might see you naked? WHO, I ask again?

My idea of camping is Holiday Inn.

Richard knows that, if I outlive him, is epitaph will read,

"He was a good husband; he never made me camp."

ALL THAT GLITTERS
CAN LEAD YOU STRAIGHT
TO THE POOR HOUSE

Hess's Department Store in Allentown, PA was my all time favorite store. A group of us started going shopping there once a year, which led to twice a year and then we were going every three months. It was the best store I ever shopped. You could buy gowns and furs, silver and china or you could shop the bargain basement. They carried high end, medium and lower priced items. They also had the best restaurant. Ask anyone who has ever been to Allentown and they most likely have eaten at the Patio Restaurant. The salads and desserts were to die for.

Yum!

One year, while doing my Christmas shopping there, I spent more than usual. On my last purchase of the day, I handed the sales clerk my gold (yes, I had a gold) card.

She entered the information into the register. Message came back "Call customer service." She called and then asked me for my driver's license (with my picture). She looked at the license, then at me and said, "Sorry, Mrs. Patrick, there has been so much activity on your card today, the computer thought it might have been stolen."

The story doesn't end there. In the Sunday a.m. sermon, the preacher was touching on the sins of the flesh, the lust of the eye, and the pride of life. He mentioned the status some people placed on gold cards issued by certain companies.

Apparently the five women who had gone shopping with me the day before had told their husbands about my incident. Heads turned my way and I heard a few of them snickering.

They were just jealous; they didn't have a gold card.

Hess's closed a number of years ago and broke the heart of lots of women.

I'LL FLY AWAY
BUT NOT ON AN AIRPLANE

I don't fly. Richard has, but isn't crazy about it. I just don't.

When I was three, a single engine plane crashed in our yard, killing the pilot.

In the 70's, a fella that I had grown up with and his wife were killed in a commercial airline accident in North Carolina.

In the 90's, my orthopedist was killed in an airplane crash.

I take that as a clear message that I should not bring added danger to the skies.

My first cousin, Barry Valentine, is past Acting Administrator for the FAA. He assures me travel by air is the safest mode of travel. When we visited him in his Washington, DC office he said, "Marilynn, you are being ridiculous. Statistically, you would have to fly every day for 19,000 years to die in an air disaster."

I just looked at him and said, "Barry, with my luck, it would be the pilot's 19,001 day on the job." I think it is very considerate of me not to jeopardize the lives of so many people.

$E = mc^2$

Thomas, (a.k.a. Running Dummy) was first time parents' poster child. He crawled at nine months, spoke in sentences by fourteen months and could do twelve piece puzzles by fifteen months.

First children evoke a sense of competition that parents never knew existed. Pediatricians and authors admonish you not to compare your child to other children, especially the first few years. They might just as well save their ink. That's wonderful advice if you have an 'ordinary' child. I challenge anyone reading this to find me a mom (or dad) who didn't compare IF their perfect angel proved to be MENSA material.

Eve must have been devastated, unable to compare Cain's accomplishments with anyone. And how did she know what to expect. Did God offer pre-natal classes and let her in on what little boys do to you when you change their diapers? Were there diapers or did he wear fig leaves? And what about feeding? Serious questions for the hereafter.

Babies have been arriving, planned or unplanned, for centuries on end. Each new parent believes that they have conceived and birthed the ultimate human being and improved on the process. Theirs is the most beautiful, smartest, happiest, toothiest, fastest, most polite child in history.

Guess what? You are so wrong. Ours was. Our Thomas.

Thomas excelled in school and was in the National Honor Society and Who's Who Among American Students. We were so proud, we failed to see what was right before our noses.

One day he dropped the bomb. He confessed to what we feared the most. We had seen all the signs but were blinded by our pride. He wanted to be an engineer. AN ENGINEER. His father's nemesis.

To say that Thomas was a bit anal was like saying Rod Blagojevich needs a hair transplant.

As I folded laundry, a daily chore with four kids, he accused me of not matching his socks correctly. I failed to see how I was matching incorrectly. They were all white (engineer, remember). I didn't get it. How can one mismatch white socks that all came out of the same twelve pack?

He grabbed three socks, laid them flat on the couch

and ordered me to examine them. Okay. I still didn't get it. Condescending would be the best word to describe how he pointed out that the big toe on two of the socks were stretched out differently than on the third. My son had a left sock and a right sock. Lord, spare me.

Thomas graduated from R.I.T. with a B.S. and Masters. As his sense of humor improved, I cut out a cartoon depicting a human resources guy interviewing a young man, nerd pack in his shirt pocket, white socks, tie stained with food, crew cut and thick glasses. The caption said it all.

"Now, let me get this straight. Are you mostly engineer or mostly human being?"

It absolutely thrills my heartstrings to pass along the word that Thomas evolved into mostly human being, thanks to a wonderful wife and two fantastic kids.

PATIENCE, THY NAME IS NOT PETE

My only sibling was a brother, six and a half years older.

One year we had a family reunion at Hilton Head; the kids, grandkids and Uncle Pete. We had three condos that each slept six. Our unit was the one where everyone chose to congregate. The doorbell buzzed constantly.

After a day or two, the adults got tired of answering it and would send one of the kids. Uncle Pete, a bachelor with no kids (thank goodness), was appalled. "How can you let those innocent children answer the door when you don't know who might be lurking on the other side? For all you know, it could be an ax murderer."

By the fourth day, when someone knocked on the door, Uncle Pete sang a different song. At that point he was yelling, "Let one of the kids go. Maybe it's the ax murderer."

TEED OFF

The consequences of Richard's deepening love for golf was the purchase of a timeshare at Marriott's Heritage Club on Hilton Head Island. Pat and Dave Halligan vacationed with us for a number of years. Rich and Dave would play golf; Pat and I would shop. A lot of great memories.

Pat had some experience playing golf but I had never played. The guys encouraged us to take lessons so we could play as a foursome.

Pat and I signed up for a ten week course. Pat got better. Alas, I did not. After the fifth lesson, the exasperated instructor took me aside and asked, very seriously, "Is someone forcing you to do this?"

I finished the ten lessons. I cannot take golf seriously. I enjoyed going out and driving the golf cart for Richard. Mostly, I enjoyed looking for golf balls lost by others. It's like a giant Easter egg hunt for adults.

ACHY, BREAKY HEART
AND OTHER BODY PARTS

Richard and I went to the same eye doctor in New York. His wife was a friend of mine and he and I shared the same birth date.

When I went in for my yearly exam, I mentioned it to him.

We discussed getting older and he remarked, "When I was young, I'd wake up in the morning and spend a few minutes in bed wondering what I was going to do that day. Now, I wake up and spend a few minutes in bed wondering what's going to hurt today."

"A" DOESN'T NECESSARILY STAND FOR APPLE

Christopher Lee Patrick was the impatient sort and arrived four to five weeks early. He brought personality and diversity to the Patricks. Chris has always had lots of friends, lots of energy, and lots of knowledge about how to drive his parents (and teachers) totally insane.

He loved being at school. He hated the work. When asked if he had any thoughts about a career, we explained that he planned to pursue a passing grade in junior high. A quick wit, he never missed an opportunity to make people laugh.

The local community college was a good option (so we thought) for him to continue his education. We were less than elated at the completion of the first semester to discover that the only thing he studied was playing cards in the cafeteria. Things improved when he paid his own tuition.

When Christopher married and moved to Florida, he decided to study reflexology and massage therapy. Imagine our surprise when he got 'A's in the classes. When had the good grades fairy Godmother waved her magic wand over his brain? And why didn't she do it ten years earlier?

Students of massage therapy are instructed that they should have the clients 'align' their auras with Uranus. The phrase tickled Christopher's ears. He shifted in his seat and said, "Wh-a-a-t?"

The teacher was not amused and advised him that he should go directly to her office after class. Ms. Sherry strode into her office, sat down and asked, "Mr. Patrick, do you know that Uranus is a planet?"

Without cracking a smirk, he came back with, "No, I knew it was big but I didn't know it was a planet."

Ms. Sherry almost choked in an attempt to stifle her vexation and chased him out of the office.

On another occasion, he was in the midst of his own personal soiree in the back of the class. The instructor posed a question. "Mr. Patrick, how are you capable of hosting your own little party in my classroom and still manage to get an 'A' on every exam?"

"I don't understand it either. It sure didn't work in high school," he retorted.

Everyone loves Chris. He is funny, affectionate and, by choice, bald.

Victoria, his daughter, will be thirteen soon. Maybe he will experience déjà vu.

I will definitely not utter those eight little words. I learned my lesson well.

RATS AND SNAILS

Lynne provided us with two grandsons. Matthew, born in 1992; Zachary, born in 1995. Matt weighed 10 lbs., 5 ozs.; Zach weighed 10 lbs., 9 ozs. We have always been extremely kind to them. We always knew they would grow up to be giants and get their revenge if we weren't. They've given us a few laughs through the years.

Mother's Day 2000, the entire Patrick clan went to a fancy restaurant for a buffet lunch. Sated, the adults relaxed at the table over coffee and dessert. Matt (already a giant at 5) wanted more food. He was permitted to go by himself. Big mistake.

The next thing we know, here comes Matthew, a big, toothless grin stretched from ear to ear. On his plate sat a huge pineapple studded with fresh fruit which HAD been the centerpiece.

Ten feet behind him, a posse of unhappy servers

were hot on his trail, yelling, "Little boy, little boy, bring that back. You can't have that. Give it to us, now."

He reluctantly gave it back, but not without a fight. We never went to that restaurant again.

Matt was fifteen and he and Zach were in the car with their father on the way to a movie. Another driver cut John off. He had to slam on brakes and the car skidded.

Matt yelled, "Be careful, Dad. I don't want to die a virgin. I have needs; my hormones are raging."

Zachary, three years younger, heard a word he didn't know and immediately wanted to know, "Ho'mones, what are ho'mones?"

EYE DROPS THAT SHOULD NOT HAVE BEEN (DROPPED)

Several summers ago, the country singer, Rodney Adkins, had a hit that was titled, "I've Been Watching You." The lyrics were about a father driving along with his young son sitting in the back seat eating after they had gone to a fast food restaurant. When the father was suddenly forced to slam on the car brakes, the jolt resulted in airborne food and a four letter word from the son's mouth.

The mortified man asked his son where he had heard that word. The kid replies, "I've been watching you, Dad."

Understandably, the father was extremely distraught and, upon arriving home, went into the barn to pray. He requests that the Lord, "Help me help my stupid self."

As we were out and about one day and the song was being played on the radio, I said to Richard, "Isn't that a great line?"

He glanced in my direction and replied, "Yeah, it sure is. I pray every day that God will help you help your stupid self."

Okay, I know some of you are appalled. You haven't lived with me. For example, a few years ago I had an eye condition (episcleritis) that required that I use three different eye drops for 10 days. In a hurry one night, I grabbed the first bottle I saw off the counter and dropped the contents in my eye. It wasn't prescribed eye drops, people. It was white-out. My eye/brain must have sensed that what was about to make contact was something that shouldn't and I partially closed my eye so it was not a full hit. My eyelashes and eyelid were covered and, since it is a natural impulse to rub the eye when a foreign body invades it, I smeared white-out all over half of my nose and face.

I looked like a mime that ran out of make-up.

MARILYNN ON BEING A MOM

The second Sunday in May is designated as Mothers' Day. It's a real big Hallmark moment. Florists, restaurants, department stores and ministers make the most of the opportunity. Have you ever gone to worship on Mothers' Day and not had a scripture read from Proverbs 31?

Of course, you haven't.

For several years, our minister had asked mothers of the congregation to share their thoughts on motherhood. Women seem to tear up and wax poetic about motherhood. I'm no different, just a bit more realistic.

Women everywhere, I would like to share my gentle thoughts with you about what it means to be a mom...

MOTHERHOOD

Nausea, throwing up, pushing pains,
Prayer.
Sleepless nights, spit up, dirty diapers,
Prayer.
Earaches, tonsillectomies, sleepless nights,
Prayer.
School days, school plays, parent-teacher conferences,
Prayer.
Sports, watching and cheering in freezing rain and snow,
Prayer.
High school, dating, cars, sleepless nights,
Prayer, prayer, prayer,
College, empty nest, sleepless nights,
Prayer
Showers, weddings, grandchildren;
God's precious cycle of life begins again.
Motherhood.
The best job on earth.

THINGS TO PONDER

There are some things that remain unanswered from our New York years; like the time Richard and Jay Hall went fishing at Little York Lake and the boat motor caught fire.

The ever thrifty (cheap) Richard and Jay liked to buy used boat motors. Richard had a small 12' john boat which they would put it on and then use it until it died a natural death. The third boat motor decided to commit suicide.

Richard drove the boat a little way out and decided that he should fill the gas tank. There was a little bit of a chop on the water that day. The gas tank opening was on the top of the motor. As Richard poured the gas in, the boat was rocking and he mananged to spill a little gas on the engine. When he went to pull the cord to start the motor, the gas ignited. Richard tried to unscrew the motor from the transom but without success. Jay

handed Richard a bucket that he had filled with water and Richard threw it on the motor. Stupidity rules. Even I know that water will cause a gas fire to spread. They decided they'd better jump. As they jumped in, the motor fell off and the fire was extinguished.

The mystery that remains unsolved is how Jay managed to stay dry from the shoulders up after jumping into the water head first. It also baffles us that Jay threw his line back into the water, hooked the motor and Richard jumped in again so they could retrieve and repair it. They stayed the rest of the day and fished. I don't pretend to understand men, but I was thankful that from that day forth, they only bought new motors.

And how did the crispy coating on Kentucky Fried Chicken disappear between the times the kids and I had supper and Richard came home from work at midnight to have his? To this day, he swears that he didn't know that KFC served breaded chicken until after the kids left home. The children insist the house was haunted and some evil spirit had a fetish for KFC.

Or how five adults and four children fit into a 1970 Mustang. My brother, Pete, and a friend came to visit us in New York but had to fly into the airport in Syracuse which was about 70 miles from Endicott. At one o'clock a.m. our car died. No service stations were open to assist us, so we decided to call our friend, Bill Woodward, to come get us. The Mustang was the only car available, and, being the good sport that he is, he came and picked us up. How nine of us survived a sixty mile ride in a car meant to seat four is still a mystery.

Pete was convinced that that particular trip ruined his chances for fatherhood.

And let us not forget the Mustard-Mobile, a huge part of Patrick lore.

The Mustard-Mobile was a 1973 Chevy truck that Richard bought in 1976. It ran great but was extremely rusted for such a fairly new truck. However, it ran like a Sherman tank. We kept the truck for fourteen years. I taught all the children to drive using it. After all, it would have been impossible to cause any body damage to it. (Remember, children, it was Mommie Dearest who taught you to drive; you owe me big. Daddy took Thomas out once and that was all he could take. (YOU OWE ME BIG!!!)

We'd be riding down the highway and parts of the truck would go flying off and be gone with the wind. Towards the end of its life, the floorboards had such big holes, we could literally see the road speeding by beneath our feet.

The Mustard-Mobile became a conversation piece for the community and people would run to get out of the way of flying debris.

In its fourteenth year with us, the truck could no longer pass state inspection. We would have to put it down. It was the end of an era and a sad day. The spirit was willing but the body wasn't able. We decided to have it cremated.

We donated our beloved Mustard-Mobile to the local volunteer fire department. They set it on fire and used it to train new firemen on how to deal with vehicular fires.

I still do not have a satisfactory answer for the next little puzzle in our life. That would be "Why me?"

In 1996, Richard went to work one morning feeling fine. About 11:00 a.m., I got a call that he'd had a massive heart attack, had gone into cardiac arrest but had been resuscitated. To sum up two months quickly, he had by-pass surgery, a brief interlude of congestive heart failure, then began to recover nicely.

That's when I began to nag him about the mess in the cellar. We had 30 years of (mostly his) junk down there and I was not going to clean it up. Forget about dying to try and get out of it. It's your mess and you will clean it up. We are talking about archery equipment and equipment to make archery equipment; golf equipment and equipment to make golf equipment; fishing rods and reels, hundreds of tools and thousands of nuts, bolts, and screws. Also, there was a john boat, waders, an old claw foot bathtub that he used as a worm bed, hunting jackets and jumpsuits, tree stands, lumber and old tires. You get the picture.

We all know that good intentions paved a very famous road…and that road ended up in my lap.

In 2005, we made the decision to sell the house and move to Florida. We no longer owned the house, it owned us and we were just tired of the responsibility and upkeep that comes with a home.

We began a "to do" list and became really excited about our new adventure. The very first thing Richard decided to do (please keep in mind that this was the FIRST thing he did) was to buy a new outdoor light fixture to place by the front door. It was lovely.

Carrying a step stool in one arm and the light fixture in the other, out the door he went to begin his project. The next thing I know, I hear a loud crash. I yell, "Richard, are you okay?" No answer. "Richard? Richard, are you alright?" Still no answer. I decided I'd better check on him. I found him lying flat on the sidewalk. The step stool had wobbled off the concrete step (which was about 24"x 48"). He was unable to move.

I called 911 and, after what seemed like hours, they arrived and took him to the hospital. Six hours later, they let us know that he had managed to break his leg into more than 300 pieces by falling directly on his knee, jamming the upper bone through his knee cap and shattering the bones below his knee cap. The doctor said that he could not have done a better job (?) with a couple sticks of dynamite.

I tell you this, my dear friends, to let you know that he found another way to get out of cleaning the @#$??*#*!! cellar. I grant you, it was an extremely gutsy way for him to do it, but it worked out well for him.

I always knew he was smarter than me. I just want to know how he came up with the plan. If it had gone awry and he had hit his head that hard, it really could have been a disaster.

And let's not forget to consider Al and Nairobi. In Chris' mind, they exist. However, the rest of us never heard of them.

All of us got together for a family reunion and Christopher asked, "Where's Al?" None of us had a clue what he meant. I asked, "Who?" He said, "Al." "Huh? Al, who?"

With a smirk on his face, he replied, "The long lost brother we never met. Remember when you broke your ankle and screamed 'Al' for three months? I thought he was a brother I didn't know about."

Al is southern speak for Ouch or, maybe, ouch is Yankee speak for al; it could be that Chris just needed his ears cleaned out.

When Richard's mom passed on in 1991, it was our responsibility to clean out her house. Richard's cousins had indicated that they would be interested in any clothing that we would be giving away. They wanted it for Nairobi.

As we went through the closets and dressers, we would indicate which boxes the items should be placed in. More often than not, Christopher was told to "put these in the box for Nairobi." On the second day, as we continued our sorting, Christopher wanted to know, "Who is this Nairobi? Is she our cousin or something?"

I would lie awake in bed at night and wonder from where in space did this child of ours come.

We're open to any ideas you might have.

By the way, you can Google Nairobi if you have questions.

Ah, sweet mysteries of life.

BIGGER FISH TO FRY

In April 2005, we moved to Florida. Because Richard was still recovering from his shattered leg, it was not an easy move. Thanks to a lot of help from children and friends, we got the job done.

We found the two things that were very important to us; a church home and a place to fish.

Dunedin is a quaint little town sandwiched between Clearwater and Tarpon Springs. There is an assortment of unique shops and restaurants, always fun to meander through.

What we like best about Dunedin is the causeway. Sometimes the fishing is good and other times it stinks. What remains constant is the assortment of people who fish there. The diversity is wonderful. If you ever get to visit, be certain to look for Lonnie, Hector, Skip, Wes, and Harry. Especially look for Harry.

Harry is a wonderfully entertaining storyteller and

will keep you laughing at his insights for a long time to come. He is called the "Mayor of the Causeway." He is 75 years old and constantly walks around picking up the trash others have not disposed of properly. Visitors frequently inquire about his ethnic background. He proudly answers the question by stating, "I'm a Native American. My ancestors were here to greet your ancestors and we've been picking up your trash ever since."

Socializing is a natural by-product of fishing. Life is good at the causeway.

Once when we were going to fish, Richard decided to make his own chum to attract the fish. He mixed squid, shrimp, sardines, oatmeal, and only God knows what else. It looked awful and smelled ten times worse. He let the creation cure for about five days and announced that it was ready and "Let's go fishing."

We loaded the rods and reels, bait and bait bucket filled with chum into the car and off we went. We were anxious to get our lines in the water and catch Jonah's whale.

We caught a few pin fish to use as bait. All things ready, Richard pulled the lid off the chum container and heaved it into the Gulf. The stench was so overpowering, I started gagging and could not stop. I walked down wind for a few minutes until the odor moved out.

We cast our lines and waited for the big boys to bite. And then, we waited some more.

A young boy was fishing off to our right and had begun to get bored by the lack of activity. He began to wander from person to person, looking at their bait or lures and just passing the time of day. He was about forty feet from his pole when suddenly there was a whi-ir-r-r-ling sound from his line. He took off at a run. Alas, it was too late. The fish on the other end of his line must have been pretty good size because it had jerked the pole from the PVC pipe pole holder and the pole was skiing across the water, last seen headed for Mexico.

Fishing caused us to catch a very serious virus; most commonly known as the boat bug. It's a very serious affliction and may impair one's common sense and good judgment. Ask us, we know. Boy, do we know.

The second happiest day in a person's life is reputed to be the day he purchases a boat. We were elated. Our eighteen foot yacht was a source of pride. Okay, it wasn't a yacht but, to us, after having owned a twelve foot john boat, it certainly seemed like one.

The book of Proverbs states that "pride goeth before the fall and a haughty spirit before destruction." Solomon owned his share of boats; he ought to know.

Every time (and I am not exaggerating) every time we put our boat in water, we wished it would sink. Oh, it (the boat) would start for the marine store, but not for us. We put it in the water four times. Every single, solitary time the motor would not catch.

The beautiful aqua and white boat would glide off the trailer into the water. A picture of dreams come true. Lake Tarpon, home to mammoth bass, would be our new playground. A mounting sense of excitement and adventure coursed through our veins.

Richard turns the key. Nothing. Again, he tries. Nothing.

He turns the key a few more times and then does the guy thing. He looks at this wire and, that connection; figuratively, he kicks the tires and taps the engine. The motor refuses to catch.

We loaded the boat back on the trailer and headed back to see our new best friends at the boat super store. We had purchased the boat from them (it was pre-owned) and they did not charge us. They knew they would be seeing us again and wanted to stay on our good side.

Our good side didn't last long.

To make a long, sad, story brief, the next three times we took the boat out, we could not get the engine to start. I'd really like for everyone to think we are smarter than we are. However, I must admit, we did not learn from our mistakes. People of reasonable intelligence and/or common sense would have recalled past outings and started the engine before they took it off the trailer and moved their vehicle to the parking area. Not us.

We needed the exercise............in stupidity.

Back to the "super" store. The reason it is named the "super" store occurred to us after our fourth and final visit. It was the super amount of cash you took out of your wallet and left with them to deposit in their super bank account.

We now understand the true definition of happiest day in your life." It's the day you sell your boat.

Amen.

Definitions for "boat."

B.O.A.T.—Bring Out Another Thousand

A bucket you set in water, fill with money, and watch float away.

SHOW ME THE WAY
TO GO HOME, PLEASE!

Most everyone agrees that grandchildren are one of the few compensations for getting older. Your own children have grown wiser and understand how stupendous you were at the parenting game that they insist that their children spend more time with you so that you can share your wisdom and knowledge with them. They are absolutely thrilled that you want to take them off their hands for two weeks.

Let's talk about our Tennessee/Branson trip with Zach and Megan. Megan is Thomas and Cindy's oldest and Zach is Lynne's youngest.

We stopped for lunch and Zach starts looking at his leg. I asked him, "What's wrong?" and he shows me two holes in his leg. One was the size of a nickel, the other, the size of a quarter. They were red, oozing, and ugly.

I immediately called Lynne and she said that Zach

had gotten bit by a spider but he said that it was okay now. HA! I told her that as soon as we stopped for the night in Cincinnati, I planned to take him to a physician.

Marriott was nice enough to help us find the closest Urgent Care Facility and off we went.

I was concerned that he might have been bitten by a brown recluse spider or might have MRSA. He had had it previously. The doctor looked at it and questioned Zach. Had you been there, you could have seen the halo around his head; he stuck to the spider bite fable. A culture was done, oral and cream antibiotics were prescribed, and we were own our way. The nurse would call us with the results of the culture.

On the road again, I can't wait to get on the road again.................Where is Willie Nelson when you need him? By mid-morning of the second day, Megan and Zach are less than thrilled with each other's company and are very testy. After all, they had nothing to do, poor babies. They only had a DVD player, CD's, Ipods, games, books, food, pillows and blankets (but did they want to sleep? I think not).

We arrived in Tennessee around five o'clock and went with our friends to a gospel meeting being held at their congregation. Richard and I loved it. Zach and Megan needed it.

It always fills our hearts with joy to visit friends and these friends had a catfish pond and big catfish.

It is an awesome sight to see hundreds of big catfish as they roil the waters in search of food.

Our last evening in Tennessee we spent at the pond trying to hook the (ever elusive) big one. As darkness and mosquitoes rested on us, we had to call it quits and headed for home. We loaded our gear and ourselves into the van and closed the doors. To be more specific, we closed three of the doors. One of the electric sliding backseat doors failed to work. At least it failed to close. The "ding, ding, ding" sound that lets you know that the door is still open worked to perfection. It "dinged" and "dinged" and "dinged." We managed to get the door closed manually but the infernal "ding" would not be silenced; nor would the interior lights go out.

This Detroit banshee shrieked till we finally arrived home. Praise God. In our naiveté, we assumed the noise would stop when the car key was removed. Never assume. Never underestimate Motor City's ability. I suspect they stay awake at night trying to find new ways to get you into dealerships to spend money (remember the super boat store).

Don, my hero, said, "No problem, I'll disconnect the battery cable tonight and you can run by the Chevy place on your way out of town tomorrow."

True to his words, Don reconnects the cable, we say our fond farewells and head to the Chevy garage. We explained our situation to the service manager. He responds, "No problem. We'll have you all set to go in a jiffy." HaHa!

Big problem. One lousy computer chip which (I'm sure you already guessed) was not in stock.

The only way to halt the incessant "ding, ding, ding" and shut off the interior lights was to remove the chip. Seemed like a simple solution. HaHaHa! This very same tiny, annoying, not in stock chip also controlled the radio, DVD player, and the CD player. AND THESE TWO LOVELY GRANDCHILDREN THOUGHT THEY HAD NOTHING TO DO BEFORE!

There is no easy way to get to Branson, Missouri from Buchanan, Tennessee. It is mostly hilly, curvy, two lane roads loaded with tractors that go too slow and trucks that go too fast down the middle of the road. In miles, you should be able to travel the distance in 5-6 hours easily. It took us nine.

A word of warning to any of you who may be making plans for a road trip to Missouri. It was our observation that the state's idea of a rest area was a port-a-john on the side of the two lane roads and a McDonald's every 100-125 miles.

Missouri is a beautiful state and Branson has more big name, live entertainment than most of us could afford to see in a week. If you go, fly.

The road trip home was a nightmare. We drove straight through and pounding or drizzling rain was our constant companion. Megan and Zach's lack of rest finally caught up to them. They did sleep most of the way home; or, I suppose, it could have been the Jack Daniels we slipped into their iced tea.

I'm kidding again, folks.

I'd love to tell you the saga ends there. Alas, we are the Patricks. Remember, nothing is simple for us. We had to take the van to the local Chevrolet dealership three times before the problem was eventually repaired. The first two replacement chips were faulty.

No problem.

THE BANJO MAN

My mother died when I was 17 and a senior in high school. As a result, my father, Thomas M. Valentine (better known as 'Monte'), and I became very close. I loved my daddy dearly but I also liked him. He was a very special man and I knew I wanted to marry a man like him. I could not have had a better example of what a husband and father should be.

That being said, I used to get mad at him for one thing in particular. He stole our boyfriends.

That didn't come out right. My best childhood friend, Carmen, lived with us for a number of months. Daddy loved to barbecue ribs. Carmen and I would invite our boyfriends to come over for dinner and they would be very attentive until Daddy got started.

Daddy played the banjo. He didn't just play; he made the banjo come alive. At that point, the guys would lose interest in us and give Daddy all the attention. I kept Richard away from him until we were married.

Daddy loved his grandbabies and they loved him. He was only 45 when Mother died and considered remarrying once after I left home and he was alone and lonely. He later told me that he was glad that he hadn't; he loved being able to spend his vacation time with us and his beloved grandbabies. Krisanne had a difficult time saying 'grandpa' when she was learning to talk and called him 'Grumpy'. He loved telling anyone who listened about being one of the seven dwarfs; Grumpy.

His banjo hung on a wall in the family room for many years.

Once we moved to Florida, we made a decision to buy cemetery plots. I decided I wanted to be buried in the town I had grown up, Haines City, where my parents were buried.

We made an appointment and made the trip to Haines City to pick out and pay for the burial plots. I wanted to be interred next to my parents but it turned out that there was only one space available. Since the ground is not conducive to "stacking" in Florida, it would be necessary to buy in another section of the cemetery. I was visibly upset and the town employee didn't know what to say to comfort me. Richard did. Richard always has the ability to put things in the proper perspective.

He simply asked, "Were you planning on having them over to dinner?"

It's a small cemetery. If they decide to come for dinner, it's not far to float.

COFFEE, TEA, OR ME?

In the spring of 2007, Richard had to have urological surgery. It was to be ambulatory surgery and he would be able to come home at the end of the day.

The procedure went according to plan and the nurse came in, gave him the discharge forms, and discussed the expected recuperation schedule.

I drove Richard home and, after he was settled in, we went over all the information again.

The only detail he questioned was the one that stated, "No sexual activity for six weeks."

With a perfectly straight face, he asked me, "Does that mean we HAVE to then?"

I KNOW A DIRTIER WORD
THAN GEORGE CARLIN

It is time for me to reiterate, yet again, that all our children are precious. Richard and I have never had to open the door to a policeman with any sort of bad news in the middle of the night; no late night calls from a hospital and only a few calls from irate teachers. Despite all the ear infections, asthma, kidney stones, broken jaws, sprained ankles and dental cavities, we have been blessed, beyond measure, with wonderful, healthy children. Some words give new meaning to "This is the day that the Lord has made. I will rejoice and be glad in it." Cancer is one of them.

On December 13th, 2007, we were broadsided with a new challenge. One we had never known, expected or wanted. Our precious daughter, Lynne, had breast cancer. She was 39 years old.

Shortly afterward, we were in the car on the way to

New York. We wanted to hold our daughter. We needed to cry with her.

We met with Lynne's surgeon and he recommended a lumpectomy and chemotherapy. He was not pleased that I thought she should have a mastectomy; he was really unhappy when I told him that I had asked her to consider a bilateral mastectomy. Lynne liked and trusted him but, well, Mom said "blah, blah, blah."

When we left New York ten days later, she was unsure what choice she would make. I never told her what she should do but asked her to check out all her options, which she did. She also spoke to several close friends who had faced breast cancer who shared their experiences with her.

In February, 2008 she had a mastectomy to remove the left breast and received chemotherapy for four months. She lost all her beautiful hair which had not been short since she was nine years old. It does not matter how many woman you have seen with cancer and hairless heads; when it is your daughter, it wallops you in the sphincter. It also allows you to see the true kindness of others.

A very special and loving thank you to all the angels who helped during Lynne's difficult times...

ANGELS

Who knew? I didn't. Did you? Who knew?

Who knew a time was coming in our lives when you would become our 'earth angels'?

We know celestial angels are God's messengers. Earth angels are God's very special servants who know saying "if there is anything I can do" is not enough. They look. They see. They do.

Paula:

When we became friends in 1971, there was no way to know the good times and the bad times we would share. We've both matured (maybe) and grown closer to each other and to God.

Thank you for your kind and loving ways. You have treated my daughter like your daughter. Thanks for all the meals, the times spent with her during chemo and, who knows how many times you drove forty-five minutes out of your way (when gas was $4 bucks a gallon) to take Zachary (the rotten kid) to school. As a mother yourself, you can understand how much this meant to us since we could not be there ourselves.

Thank you.

Tracy:

Who knew when we met a long time ago, that this awful, horrible disease would bring us together again? I had heard from a mutual friend that you had also had breast cancer and was uncertain if it would be okay to call you. I'm so glad I did.

Thank you for being the compassionate sister to Lynne when her own sister could not be there to help her through the difficult days, weeks, and months ahead. You had first-hand knowledge of what she was enduring. As much as we all loved her, we did not have that insight. Thanks for all you have done and continue to do for her.

Linda and Jim:

Who knew when Lynne began the job with Belknap Lumber that she would find such wonderful, supportive people. We have been overwhelmed by your kindnesses. Thanks to everyone who shaved their heads to support Lynne. BALD IS BEAUTIFUL!

Thank you for your empathy, patience and charity in allowing Lynne to have the time off that she needed. We will be forever grateful for your generosity to Lynne so that she did not have to worry about food, housing, AND cancer. Linda, Jim, you are very special people.

We encounter so many individuals in our lives. Some remain acquaintances, some become friends and, a very special few, become 'Donnas'.

Donna:

Who knew when we met in the early '70's what the future might bring? We visited in each other's homes a few times and spent time together at church events; after a few years, you moved back to North Carolina. Our friendship might have evolved into the yearly Christmas letter. It has not only withstood the test of time; it has withstood the test of distance.

You have always had a tender, caring, charitable heart but Lynne's struggle further confirmed what we already knew. You don't preach; you practice. Thank you for the liberal gift you gave Lynne to help with her medical expenses. It was a great blessing.

Who knew? God knew. He knows our yesterdays, our todays and our tomorrows. He knew the first day we said, "Hello" that a day would come that a terrifying disease would unite us in a very special way.

He knew that Richard and I would sleep better at night knowing that all of you were there to help Lynne and her boys. You made bearable the seemingly unbearable.

We love you, true friends. You are all special gifts from God.

Earth angels.

KEEP A GOOD THOUGHT
AND PRAY HARD

Lynne finished the chemotherapy June 26th, 2008. She was scheduled for a mammogram on her right breast in August. The results, once again showed abnormal tissue and a biopsy was scheduled.

Thank God, the tissue was benign, but she had had enough. She opted for a second mastectomy.

Since I would be off work the week of Thanksgiving, she scheduled the surgery for November.

The Patrick baseball game of life was about to get hit by a 105 mile an hour curve ball pitch.

AND THE WINNER IS...

Just before Lynne's mastectomy in October, Richard won the lottery. The only problem is we didn't buy a ticket and it wasn't a lottery anyone wants to win.

Richard had been having sinus problems for six months. He had been to our family doctor and had been given decongestants, antibiotics, steroids and nothing had done any good.

Our doctor made an appointment with an ENT (think HMO). The man had no personality.

He did do an x-ray and told Richard that he would require surgery to remove polyps.

Richard had already had this type of surgery ten years before. Nasty surgery but everything was fine.

Richard also goes to the VA (which is absolutely wonderful). His GP set up an appointment with the ENT there who arranged for surgery. We liked the doctor very much and techniques had improved so he wasn't so miserable this time.

Fast forward a week. The doctor calls and tells Richard that the pathology report showed something but the three pathologists who had looked at it could not agree on what. It was cancer but they didn't know what kind.

Dr. Merchant advised us that the tissue has been sent to Bethesda Naval Hospital to the most renown pathologist in the world.

I left for NY with a heaviness of heart. I didn't want Richard to have to face this alone but Lynne and the boys needed me during surgery and recovery.

The only upside for this trip was that my Florida granddaughter, Victoria Blessing Patrick, would be traveling with me. It was to be her first train trip and the first time she would see snow. It was also the first opportunity I had ever had to spend a prolonged period of time with her. We enjoyed getting to know each other better and getting to visit with other people on the trip. I love trains. The dining car is still a very special event.

Dear friends, Jacque Horbey and her son, Stephen, picked us up in Philadelphia and drove us back to Endicott. It was a bonus getting to spend the evening with them.

Good old Richard. I truly wish every woman (especially my daughters) could have a husband like him. He called me to tell me that it was sinus cancer. According to the statistics I read on the internet, only .75 per 100,000 people ever get sinus cancer. He apparently has the rarest form.

He is currently in the process of receiving 30 radiation treatments.

I am so thankful for a family with a good sense of humor and strong faith. The oncologist told Richard that he might lose the hair in his nose. I asked if he could give him a little more radiation so he could lose the hair in his ears. Lynne told him not to worry; she'll loan him her wig for his head.

He called me in New York and asked me if I would make him a wig to replace the hair in his nose.

PERKS

The physician who had performed Lynne's first mastectomy had retired. We were very pleased with the doctor who attended Lynne for the removal of the right breast. Dr. Muhich, a woman, is much more in tune with the emotional upheaval of these kinds of decisions. Dr. Walker had performed the first breast implant and would do this one also. Dr. Walker is a hoot. A great doctor, but a real hoot. I may have to wash his mouth out with soap.

Lynne and the good doctor occasionally get into shouting matches. It's all in good fun but they both say exactly what they think. After one visit when he accused Lynne of overdoing and yelled at her, she planned her revenge.

On her next visit, when he lifted the gown to example his handiwork, he was surprised to see tattoos of Eeyore where nipples should have been. Don't panic. They were temporary tattoos.

Lynne had a total of six surgeries and eight chemotherapy treatments in 2008. She has two more surgeries scheduled for this year and then will have to decide if she will have nipples tattooed on her implants so they will look more natural. Yes, they really do tattoo nipples on.

One of Lynne's friends, Hugh, proposed to her after the first surgery. He told her he thought that she was the perfect woman and she had all the attributes any man would look for in a wife. She was smart, funny, pretty and would always have one perky breast.

Now, she will always have two.

SO, SUE ME ALREADY

I absolutely love living in the age of frivolous lawsuits. Remember the woman who went to McDonald's drive-up window, ordered hot coffee, placed the cup between her legs and merrily went on her way. Well, maybe not so merrily. For whatever reason, the coffee sloshed out, burned her legs and she sued McDonald's because the coffee was too hot. She was awarded millions for what I choose to call stupidity.

Enter a doctor who resides in New York. A recent article in the newspaper reported that he is suing his soon-to-be ex-wife so he can get back the kidney that he had previously donated to her. The news column stated that the woman had undergone two previous transplants, which her body rejected. Her husband donated one of his kidneys and the transplant was successful.

As a matter of fact, the transplant was so successful

that she was able to attend a fitness center. She's lookin' good; she's feelin' good. Her life is back on track. Unfortunately, like so many of us, she derailed it. She met a fitness instructor at the center and began an affair.

Uh-oh. Dr. Husband is justifiably miffed and he wants his kidney returned. Certainly, there was no shortage of attorneys itching to grab their fifteen seconds of fame.

I've got a microscope on this lawsuit. If Dr. Husband wins, I'm gonna sue Richard to get my virginity back. Know any good lawyers?

SPIDER BITE REVISITED

I've kept you in suspense long enough. The time has come to speak of many things; mainly Zachary and the hideous holes.

Kids. Rotten kids!!!

Zachary did not have a spider bite. Zachary did not have MRSA. Zachary did not get born with a brain.

Matthew finally spilled the beans (or, perhaps, the BB's). Trust older brother to rat you out. Our beloved grandson had accidentally shot himself in the leg with his BB gun. He knew that if he told his Mom what he had done, he would be in big trouble; ala Al Gore, it would be "An Inconvenient Truth." He did what every red blooded American boy would do. He dug the BB out of his leg with a knife and concocted the spider bite tale. Now he has two wounds to explain; a large wound (quarter size) where the BB entered and a smaller wound (nickel size) where he dug it out. How can you have the guts to take a knife and dig a hole in your OWN leg and not have the courage to tell your Mom what you did?

Parents experience a wide range of emotions when something like this occurs. First, we are thankful that he didn't hit an artery or require surgery to remove the BB; second, comes anger; next, the guilt sets in for allowing yourself to be talked into buying him the gun, despite the sincere promises that he would be careful. Finally, you realize that blood is thicker than water and he probably takes after Grandma.

"Lord, help them help them stupid selves.

Amen.

OPEN MY EYES, LORD

Have you ever been struck with a moment of total clarity? I'm not talking about déjà vu. It's like the proverbial light bulb is switched on over your head and its beam is 500 watts. Strange experience.

The coffee pot spitted and spurted in the kitchen as morning's magical elixir permeated the room with life's most desired a.m. beverage. The TV was tuned to an early morning news show. The anchor introduced a fisherman from New Zealand who had a unique way to catch fish. Poor soul no longer cared to fish like everyone else. He had a new "hook" on this ancient sport. I'm sure his mother must be very proud.

He boards a helicopter in search of a large fish. Once a suitably sized fish is spotted, he positions himself to jump out and land on top of the fish and wrestles it to submission.

A film clip was aired providing proof that he jumped

out and onto the back of a marlin (visualize a big fish with a long tail).

The clueless anchor inquired, "Isn't that dangerous?"

His response to the question provided me with something to think about. "No, not really. People think that because they are big, they are dangerous. The truth is that, even though they are big, they have very small brains and are only fixated on eating."

Hello, light bulb. Hello, clanging bells. Hello, marching bands. The moment of clarity struck me as sharply as a bolt of lightning!

I'm big; I have a small brain; and I'm fixated on eating. I'M A FISH!!!!!

TOGETHER AGAIN

At the end of February 2009, Richard finished the radiation. We let out a sigh of relief and our excitement was contagious for an upcoming family reunion. We would all be together again for the first time in four years.

Richard had an appointment with his primary care physician in late March for blood work. It was routine. Routine? After 65, none of us should ever expect tests/exams to be routine. Let's face it. We start failing more tests in the doctor's office than we ever did in high school. He got a call a few days later that his PSA numbers were elevated and needed more tests. To spare you the details, I'll just say it. He had prostate cancer.

He was not scheduled to see the doctor regarding surgery, radiation or chemotherapy until after our family reunion. We planned to make memories with our children and grandchildren and enjoy our time together.

We met half of our expectations. We made memories.

Read on.

WE ARE FAMILY

Our family reunion rolled every stereotyped bad movie/sitcom into an extravaganza that paled anything Hollywood has to offer:

Day One—Smiling faces, hugs, kisses, excited voices making plans for the week.

Day Two—Breakfast together; bright eyes, bathing suits, towels; high hopes. Clearwater Beach, here we come.

Day Three—Lazy day by the pool, mild breeze, warm sun. Life is good.

Day Four—Sunburned arms; sunburned backs; sunburned legs. Raccoon eyes and Rudolph noses. Life sucks.

Day Five—Tempers erupt. Angry looks, angry kids, angry parents. Hurt feelings.

Day Six—Regrets; embarrassment; sheepish smiles. 'Last night' dinner.

Day Seven—Early morning departures; tear-filled eyes; Lots of 'I love you(s). Home to New York; home to Texas.

Day Eight—Mom (Grandma), Dad (Grandpa), worn out, reclining in their Lazy Boys. Contours plumped to fit shape of their bodies.

DAMN FAMILY REUNIONS.

IT'S YOUR TURN NOW, DR. WALKER

The latest visit Lynne made to Dr. Walker brought a new meaning to a holiday wish list.

She told him, "All I want for Christmas are my two front teats."

Hopefully, the tattooing will be done by then and this phase of her life will come to an end.

HAIR TODAY,
GONE TOMORROW

Richard began a series of 43 radiation treatments for prostate cancer in May. He has seven more before they will be completed. He has experienced unusual fatigue as a result of the radiation. I don't know if he has lost any hair this go round or not. We haven't spoken about it since I told him that if he did lose hair and needed a wig, this time he was on his own. Any hair lost this time is between him and the doctor.

Cancer is not amusing, but we have retained our ability to laugh and find humor in our circumstances. We decided to get a rescue dog to be a companion for Richard while I work. Jethro Gibbs (this maltipoo is as close as I will ever get to Mark Harmon of NCIS). This wonderful little dog has brought a new dimension to our lives.

He owns us. Remember the old Kennel Ration jingle, "My dog is better than your dog. My dog is better than yours." Need I say more?

OUT OF THE MOUTH
OF MARILYNN

July 12, 2009. How oddly appropriate that I write the final reminiscence today. It is our 45th anniversary.

In all the years, we never considered divorce. We considered murder many times. We were brought up in era when God forgave murder but not divorce.

I would encourage you, dear friends, young or not so young. Keep the humor in your marriage. Never marry anyone you don't like or respect. And let us put the sexual aspect into perspective. The pleasure is temporary and the position is ridiculous.

Love is an account you should always deposit into and withdraw from but it should certainly accumulate interest. Many wrongs turns will be taken but, remember, always remember, that on this adventure, one of you always knows how to get there and the other knows how to get home.

Have a wonderful journey.

CORN CHOWDER

6 sliced bacon, cut into 1" pieces
3 tblsp butter
3 large onions
¼ cup flour
1 46 oz can chicken broth
1 pkg frozen hash brown potatoes
3 10 oz. pkg frozen whole kernal corn
1 each red and green pepper, diced
½ tsp black pepper
1 ½ cup half and half

Cook bacon in Dutch oven until crisp. Remove and add butter; melt. Add onions and peppers and cook till tender. Add chicken broth and potatoes. Bring to boil, stirring to loosen the bits from bottom of pan. Reduce heat and simmer for 15 minutes or until potatoes are tender.

Add corn and black pepper. Simmer 8-10 minutes. Add half and half. Heat through but do not boil. Serve into bowls and sprinkle crumbled bacon on top.

SAUERKRAUT SOUP

1 quart broth from ham bone OR 3 Pork Ramen
Noodles Flavor Packs
1 26 oz. can cream of mushroom soup
1 large can sauerkraut (to rinse or not to rinse, it's up to
you)
6 cups cooked, diced potatoes or use Ore-Ida potatoes
O'Brien

Mix broth and mushroom soup. Bring to boil. Add
sauerkraut. Simmer at least 30 minutes.

Fry potatoes as you would for home fries. Ladle soup
into bowls and pass home fries so that guest can add
amount wanted to soup.

Soup can be simmered for five minutes and placed in
refrigerator overnight. We think the taste is better after
being refrigerated and reheated.

Yum! Yum!

BEST EVER SPINACH SALAD

1 bag spinach
1 small chopped red onion
8 slices bacon, cooked and crumbled

OPTIONAL
1 can water chestnuts
1 can bean sprouts
fresh mushrooms

DRESSING
¾ cup salad oil
¼ cup white or wine vinegar
½ cup sugar
1 tblsp worchestire sauce
salt and pepper to taste

Mix vegetables, toss with dressing, and add bacon.
I usually leave out the bean sprouts, mushrooms, and water chestnuts.
Most frequently, I will add smoked turkey breast and hot pepper cheese.

BROCCOLI CAULIFLOWER SLAW

1 pkg fresh broccoli florets
1 pkg fresh cauliflower florets
12 slices cooked and crumbled bacon (or 1 jar of Bacon Bits)
1 small red onion, chopped
½ cup sunflower seeds
1 cup raisins or dried cranberries
1 cup mayonnaise
½ cup sugar
2 tablespoons vinegar

Chop broccoli and cauliflower into small pieces. Add next four ingredients. Stir mayo, sugar and vinegar together until smooth and pour over slaw. Add salt and pepper if desired.

SUMMER SQUASH CASSEROLE

This recipe is probably the all time favorite Patrick recipe; it's simple to make and great to eat. I suggest you serve it with lots of cornbread. Southern cooking doesn't get any better than this.

8 slices bacon, cooked and crumbled
4-6 summer squash (depending on size)
1 large onion
4-6 fresh tomatoes (depending on size) peeled
Velveeta cheese, sliced
Salt and pepper to taste

Fry bacon in a skillet. Set aside. Pour off the bacon grease from frying pan but DO NOT wipe out or rinse pan. Wash vegetables. Slice squash into bottom of fry pan. Top with sliced onions. Cook for 10-15 minutes or until tender. Top with sliced tomatoes and continue cooking for another 10-15 minutes. Use spatula to press vegetables down to extract broth to keep from sticking. When veggies are tender, cover with sliced Velveeta cheese and crumbled bacon. Cover and continue cooking until cheese has melted.

Serve with favorite cornbread. Yum! Yum!

CHICKEN AND FLAT DUMPLINGS (SOUTHERN)

1 whole fryer, or 4-5 chicken breast OR 6-10 thighs (we prefer thighs) Place in large (no stick) pot and season with salt, pepper, garlic, Season All, etc. Bring to boil and simmer until done. Remove from pot, cool and debone. Place back in broth and add 46 ounces of canned chicken broth. Bring to boil and simmer.

Meantime, make dumplings. Like most Southern woman before me, there are many dishes that do not have recipes. You go by the look and feel of the dough. This is one of them. Listed ingredients are approximate but, most of you probably have good sense, judge for yourselves when the dough is no longer sticky and can easily be rolled out like pie crust.

4-5 cups of regular flour
½ tsp salt
½ teaspoon black pepper
½ teaspoon paprika
Chicken broth as needed (I use Campbell's)

Sift dry ingredients together into a large bowl. Add chicken broth until dough becomes workable on a floured surface. Pour 1-1/2 cups flour on work surface and place dough on top of flour. Turn dough to coat all sides. To avoid tough dumplings, allow the dough to rest 10-15 minutes before rolling into a rectangle. Roll into thickness of a pie crust; cut into 1" to 2" squares, depending on your patience. Place in boiling broth and cook 15-20 minutes.

If you eat immediately after dish is fully cooked, you will have thin dumplings and lots of broth. Once dumplings cool and absorb more broth, they become thicker and dryer. To reheat, additional broth should be added.

KOLACHI

½ lb Philadelphia cream cheese
½ cup margarine
2 cups flour

Mix above three ingredients thoroughly. Divide into three balls. Wrap and chill (can keep overnight).

Roll out in 10X sugar and cut into 4" wide strips. Spread with filling and roll up. Cut rolled pastry into 1" strips and bake at 325 degrees for 15-20 minutes or until bottom is brown.

Solo almond and apricot fillings work very well. Just remember not to spread to close to edge.

WALNUT FILLING

2 cups finely chopped walnuts
½ cup sugar
1 tsp orange zest (or 1 tsp orange juice)
1 egg white
2 tsps vanilla
¼ tsp milk

Mix and refrigerate until ready to use.

MOTHER'S PECAN PIE

3 eggs
1 cup white Karo syrup
½ cup white sugar
½ tsp salt
1 tsp vanilla
1 cup chopped pecans

Mix all together and pour into unbaked pie crust. Bake at 350 degrees 45-55 minutes or until set.